About the book

All over the world, people have been making masks for thousands of years. The masks were made from animal hides and fur, stone, wood, metal, shells, cloth and even corn husks. The mask makers would use whatever materials they could find in the areas where they lived. Masks were worn for many reasons such as disguise, protection, religious ceremonies, entertainment and festive holidays. Monster masks are fun to wear and make. They also make decorative wall hangings. The masks in this book are easy to make from materials readily found either in your house or in local stores. Be inventive when making your masks as were the mask makers throughout history.

EASY·TO·MAKE

MONSTER MASKS
AND DISGUISES

written and illustrated by Frieda Gates

PRENTICE-HALL, INC. • **ENGLEWOOD CLIFFS, N.J.**

Thanks to my mask makers,
especially Kat and Tris

Easy To Make Monster Masks and Disguises
824   by Frieda Gates
Copyright © 1979 by Harvey House, Publishers
Treehouse Paperback edition published 1981 by Prentice-Hall,
Inc. by arrangement with Harvey House, Publishers

Printed in the United States of America • J
10 9 8 7 6 5 4 3 2 1
Library of Congress Cataloging in Publication Data
Gates, Frieda.
Easy to make monster masks and disguises.
Reprint. Originally published: New York:
Harvey House, 1979.
Summary: Instructions for making masks and disguises from
a variety of materials.
1.   Masks–Juvenile literature.   [1.   Masks.
2.   Handicraft]   I.   Title.
TT898.G38   1981   731'.75   81-5955
ISBN 0-13-222794-0   AACR2

CONTENTS

PLAIN PAPER MASK

Materials & Tools: paper, pencil, crayons or markers, scissors, string

1. Hold the paper over your face to feel and draw eye holes.
2. Draw the face of a monster, a person or an animal.
3. Cut out the face shape, eye holes, a nose flap and an opening for your mouth.
4. Poke holes, and tie strings to each side of the mask.

Instead of strings, tape a stick either at the bottom or on one side of the mask.

A paper plate can also be used to make a mask.

ORIGAMI MASK

Origami is the ancient Japanese art of paper folding.

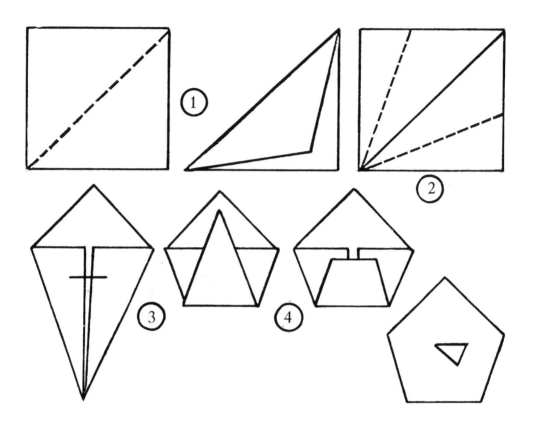

Materials & Tools: paper (15″ square), pencil, scissors, tape, string, coloring tools.

1. Fold paper as shown.
2. Unfold paper and turn sides to a kite shape.
3. Cut a slit as indicated.
4. Fold up the bottom and insert the tip into the slit.
5. Hold the mask in front of your face and find your eyes. Mark these spots. Cut out eye holes.
6. Draw and color an ugly monster face, or a person with a pointy nose.
7. Put small pieces of tape on each side of the mask. Poke holes through the tape and tie strings onto the mask.

SCULPTURED PAPER MASKS

A mouse, a cow, a make-believe animal and a monster.

Materials & Tools: paper (18″ x 12″), scissors, stapler, paint.
1. Cut on the solid lines.
2. Fold on the broken lines.
3. Staple together at x marks.
4. Paint the mask or leave it as is.
Try to create other masks using this method.

PAPER BAG MASKS

Materials & Tools: grocery bag, crayons or paint, scissors.
1. Place the grocery bag over your head and feel where your eyes, nose and mouth are. Mark these spots.
2. Remove the bag. Cut out eye holes, breathing holes or a nose flap and an opening for your mouth.
3. Draw and color a friendly face or an angry face.
4. Trim or fold the bottom of the bag so it will fit comfortably.

PAPER BAG MONSTER MASK — a paper bag with additions.
Materials & Tools: large grocery or shopping bag, black plastic
bag, egg carton scissors, glue, cellophane tape, crayons.
1. Place the bag over your head. Feel where your eyes are and
   mark these spots.
2. Remove the bag and cut nostril holes where your eyes will be.
3. Cut egg cup eyes from the egg carton. Draw eyeballs.
4. Glue the egg cup eyes onto the bag. Draw a mouth.
5. Cut the plastic bag into strips about 6″ long and ½″ wide.
6. Tape the strips all over the bag to look like monster hair.

CYLINDER MASK

Materials & Tools: heavy paper or posterboard: the length should be long enough to fit around your head but the height is optional (see step #3), glue, tape or stapler, coloring tools, colored construction paper.

1. Roll and attach the edges of the paper to form a cylinder. Tape or staple it together.
2. Place the cylinder over your head. Mark eyes and nose with x marks. Cut out the eye holes and a nose flap.
3. Either have a tall head mask or trim it to a shorter size. Strips can be cut at the top or bottom to make hair or a beard. The strips can be bent to curl.
4. Draw and color a face, or glue on colored paper to shape features. **This mask can be a monster or** . . . . .

A man with a top hat:

5. Place the cylinder on a piece of black paper, and draw the outline of the oval shape of the cylinder. Draw another oval about 3″ wider. Draw tabs as shown. This is a hat brim.
6. Cut out the brim and slip it over the cylinder. Tape the tabs above the face.
7. Measure the height of the hat and cover it with black paper.
8. Cut out black paper brows, a moustache and a beard. Tape them to his face.
9. For his curly haired wife, cut strips and bend to curl them. Tape on paper earrings.

CONEHEAD MONSTER MASK

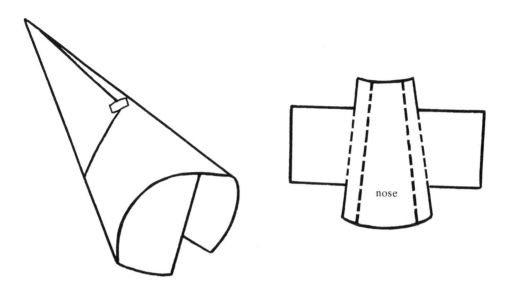

Materials & Tools: posterboard (21″ x 25″), white plastic dairy container, colored construction paper, pencil, scissors, glue, tape.

1. Bend to form the posterboard into a cone shape. Tape or glue the edges to hold it together.
2. Trim the bottom of the cone to fit comfortably on your shoulders. Find comfortable eye holes and mark these spots.
3. Cut out eye holes and slits for the nose and a mouth. Cut slits at the top for paper hair.
4. Draw a nose shape with tabs (as shown) from the trimmed off posterboard.
5. Insert and tape the nose tabs in slits. Tape the tabs to the inside of the mask.
6. Make teeth from the plastic container. Tape the teeth onto the mask on the reverse side of the mouth slit.
7. Cut out eyes and brows and strips for hair from colored construction paper.
8. Glue on eyes and brows. Remember to leave eye holes. Bulging eyes can be made from an egg carton.
9. Insert strips for hair in slits. Tape them on the inside of the mask. The ends can be rolled and curled.

CREPE PAPER MASK

Materials & Tools: package of brightly colored crepe paper, colored construction paper, glue, tape.

1. Wrap the crepe paper around your head, gathering the paper together at the top. Lift the paper off and tape it together at the top and at the back.
2. Put the mask back on and find your eyes. Mark these spots.
3. Cut out eye holes. You may also cut a mouth opening and a nose flap or breathing holes.
4. Cut out features from colored paper and glue them on. Cut streamers at the top or add crepe paper hair.
5. You can add texture by stretching the paper with your fingers. This could produce ugly bumps on a monster head.

FITTED CARDBOARD MASK

Materials & Tools: cardboard, pencil, scissors, bowl of water, large bottle (such as a 1½ gallon bleach bottle), string paint.

1. Draw and cut a mask shape out of cardboard. Design the mask in any shape you want.
2. Soak the mask in a bowl of water until it is soft.
3. Wrap and tie the mask around the bottle. A nose can be shaped by placing an object under the nose area.*
4. Remove the mask when it is dry. Hold the mask to your face and find your eyes. Mark these spots. Cut out eye holes.
5. Draw and paint a face. Make the face scary or funny.
6. Poke holes and insert strings to hold the mask over your face.

* A wad of paper rolled into a ball was placed under this mask.

CARDBOARD MONSTER MASK

Materials & Tools: large piece of cardboard (the kind used for cartons), 2 8-ounce dairy containers (such as yogurt) with tops, pencil, scissors, tape, glue, twine, wooden stick, paper, black marker or crayon.

1. Draw and cut out a large mask shape. It can be round, oval, square or any shape you design.

2. Cut out a square mouth. Make the mouth large enough to see out of.

3. Cut one of the containers in half as shown. Cover the container with paper and tape it together at the back. Glue it on the mask to be a nose.

4. Glue the dairy container tops on for eyes. Draw eyeballs with a black crayon or marker.

5. Cut out teeth from the other container. Glue them into the mouth on the reverse side of the mask.

6. Poke holes around the outer edge of the mask. Cut twine into 12″ lengths. Insert and tie the twine in the holes around the mask.

7. Tape a wooden stick on the reverse side, at the bottom of the mask. Hold the stick to cover your face with the mask.

You should be able to see out of the monster's mouth.

BAS-RELIEF MASK

Bas-relief is a term in sculpture meaning a slightly raised design on a flat surface.

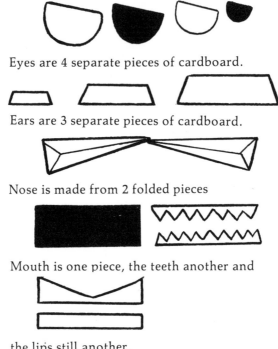

Eyes are 4 separate pieces of cardboard.

Ears are 3 separate pieces of cardboard.

Nose is made from 2 folded pieces

Mouth is one piece, the teeth another and

the lips still another.

Materials & Tools: corrugated cardboard (type cartons are made of), scissors, pencil, glue, 2 wooden sticks, paint.

1. Design and cut a large shape out of cardboard for the base. Cut out an area to see out of. It does not have to be out of the eyes of the mask.

2. Cut out shapes for features. Glue pieces of cardboard, one on top of the other, placed under the features to make them stand out.

3. Corrugated cardboard can be peeled apart, cut into strips and curled. Use peeled pieces to add texture to the brows, hair or anywhere else on your mask.

4. Glue 2 wooden sticks at the bottom of the mask, on the reverse side.

5. Paint the mask using bright colors.

COMPOSITE MASK

A composite mask means that this mask is made up of a variety of things.

Materials & Tools: large pieces of posterboard or cardboard, pencil, scissors, glue, tape, decorations (see step #3).

This should be a large mask.

1. Hold the board over your face and find the areas for your eyes. Mark these spots. Draw the head shape.
2. Cut out the head shape and the eye holes. Breathing holes and a mouth opening may also be cut.
3. Decorate this mask with any combination of colored paper, foil, egg carton, feathers, string, twine, yarn, straw, beads, fabric, paper clips, pipe cleaners, buttons, bottle caps, sequins and anything else you can find to attach. Paint may also be added.
4. Be sure the mask is not made too heavy to wear. Poke holes on each side of the mask. Tie strings to each side. Tie the strings together at the back of your head.

Masks that are made too heavy to wear can be used as interesting wall hangings.

This mask is made up of the following:
Hair — yarn
Eyes — small pie plates.
Eyeballs — felt and bottle caps
Nose — gourd
Teeth — egg carton
Whiskers — pipe cleaners
Freckles — sequins
Horns — cardboard covered with foil

BOXHEAD MONSTER MASKS

Materials & Tools: any size box that will fit comfortably over your head, pencil, scissors, paint or colored construction paper.
1. Cut out the bottom of the box. If the box reaches past your shoulders, cut half circles from the sides to fit over your shoulders.
2. Place the box on your head and mark spots for eye holes. Cut out eye holes.
3. Draw an ugly monster face. A used light bulb or a balloon nose can be inserted in a hold in the box head. Paper cups can be taped or glued on for ears. See what else you can find to use.
4. Paint or glue on colored construction paper for other features.
5. Yarn or an old mop can be used for hair.
Robot Monster:
Cover the box head with aluminum foil, use black tape for features, attach pipe cleaners for antennae and insert a light bulb nose.

Ears are small pie plates glued on the sides of the Box-head.

PAPIER MÂCHÈ MASK

Papier mâché objects have lasted for more than 2,000 years.
For the paste mixture you may use flour, cornstarch, wheat or library paste. Combine any of these with water to make a creamy mixture.

Materials & Tools: newspaper, paste mixture, tape, paper cup, egg carton, 2 dairy containers with tops, pail of water, mixing bowl, scissors, paint, string.

1. Tear several sheets of newspaper into strips around 1″ wide. Soak the strips in a pail of water. Set it aside.
2. Roll 2 or 3 sheets of dry newspaper into a long tube shape. Tape it to hold it together. Shape the tube to the oval of your face. This is the frame of the mask.
3. Crush a ball of dry newspapers and fit it inside the frame.
4. Cover the crushed newspaper and frame with 2 sheets of dry newspaper. Tuck and tape these sheets to the back edges of the frame. The crushed newspaper should be removable.
5. Prepare paste mixture in a bowl.
6. Cut 2 egg carton cups for eyes. Place them on top of the dry newspaper. Squeeze excess water from the soaking newspaper strips. Dip strips into the paste, remove excess paste and cover the egg carton eyes. Repeat this process, using a paper cup for a nose and dairy containers, bottom side up, for cheeks, (trim the containers so they lay lower than the nose). Use one container top for a mouth, and cut the other container top in half to add ears. Mold the face with more strips.
7. Allow the mask to dry for a day or more. Cut out eye holes, and paint the face of a monster or a clown.
8. Attach strings.

— Method No. 1

Step #2

Step #3

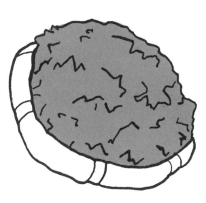

The monster has sharp teeth cut from a dairy container.

The sad clown wears a paper cone hat.

PAPIER MÂCHÈ MASK

Materials & Tools: plasticine, paste mixture (see papier mâché method #1), sculpting tools, bowl 6″ wide and 3″ deep, vaseline, plastic wrap, pail of water, mixing bowl, scissors, paint, string.

1. Tear newspapers into strips, around 1″ wide. Soak strips in the pail of water. Set it aside.
2. Turn the bowl upside down. Place a sheet of plastic wrap over the bowl. Cover the bowl with a layer of plasticine. Use more plasticine to shape features.
3. Cover the mold with vaseline.
4. Prepare paste mixture in the mixing bowl.
5. Squeeze excess water from the soaking newspaper strips. Dip the strips into the paste, remove excess paste and cover the mold. Use 3 or 4 layers. Allow the mask to dry for a day or more before removing it from the mold.
6. Cut out eye holes. Paint the face. Attach strings.

For the mask shown, you will need an old sheet or cloth, a strip of red felt (2″ wide and 7″ long) and paint.

Cut the sheet into long strips and glue them to the top of the mask for very long hair. The hair can hang down to the floor.

The strip of red felt should be cut into the shape of a long tongue. Make a slit in the mouth and insert the tongue.

Tape the end of the tongue to the back of the mask. Paint the face using very bright colors.

— Method No. 2, using a mold

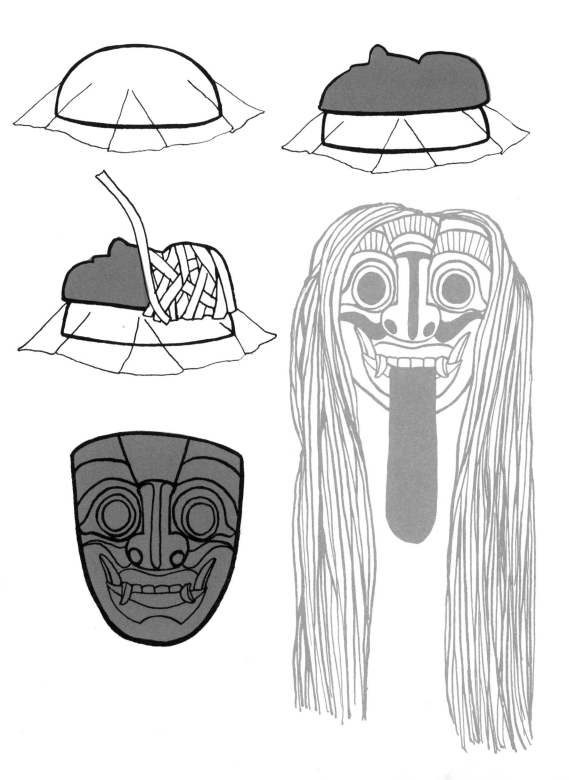

CLOTH MÂCHÈ MASK

Materials & Tools: plasticine, rags cut into strips, white glue, water, container for mixing glue, sculpting tools, scissors, bowl 6″ wide and 3″ deep, plastic wrap, paint, vaseline.

1. Turn the bowl upside down and place a sheet of plastic wrap over the bowl.
2. Cover the bowl with a layer of plasticine. Use more plasticine to shape features.
3. Cover the mold with vaseline.
4. Thin glue with water.
5. Dip rags strips in the glue mixture and cover the plasticine. Allow the mask to dry for a day or more.
6. Remove the plasticine when the mask is completely dry.
7. Cut out eye holes and paint the mask.

Decorate your mask by gluing on feathers, colorful yarn, sparkles or anything else you can find.

GAUZE MÂCHÈ MASK *

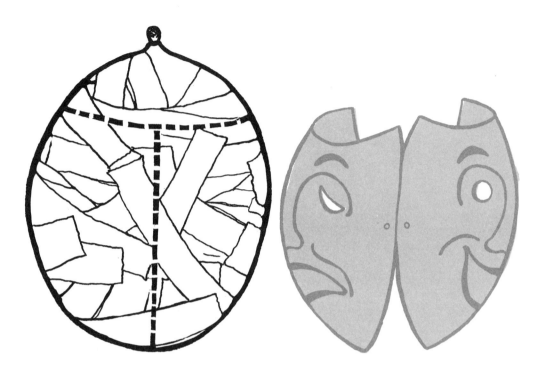

Materials & Tools: gauze, (bought at any supermarket or drug store), white glue or papier mâché paste mixture, brush (an inch or more in width), a balloon at least the size of your head, empty juice can, mixing bowl, scissors, paint, string.

1. Mix paste mixture or thin the glue with water in the bowl.
2. Blow up the balloon. Tie it tightly. Place it in the juice can to hold it steady.
3. Dip your brush in the mixture and coat the balloon. Layer the gauze over the balloon. Coat each layer with the mixture, and overlap the strips. Use about 3 layers.
4. Let the covering dry for a day or more.
5. Cut the covering in half. Paint a face on each mask. Cut out mouth and eye holes. Attach strings.

* Gauze mâché is lighter than paper or cloth and by using a balloon, you can make 2 masks at once.

CLOTH HOOD MONSTER MASK

Materials & Tools: old pillow case*, scissors, pencil, glue, fabric scraps, old sock, yarn, needle and thread.

* If you don't have an old pillow case, cut 2 sides from a piece of fabric and sew them together to make a hood.

1. Place the pillow case over your head. The pillow case can be worn with corners creating ears or one corner creating a point at the top. Feel where your eyes, nose and mouth are. Mark these spots.
2. Cut out eye holes and an opening for your mouth.
3. Cut the fabric scraps in shapes for features. Glue or sew them on the hood. Make the features scary or funny.
4. Cut the toe portion of an old sock off. Stuff it and sew it on for a nose. Use a colorful sock.
5. Yarn can be glued or sewn on for hair, brows, or a moustache and beard.

PLASTIC BOTTLE MASK

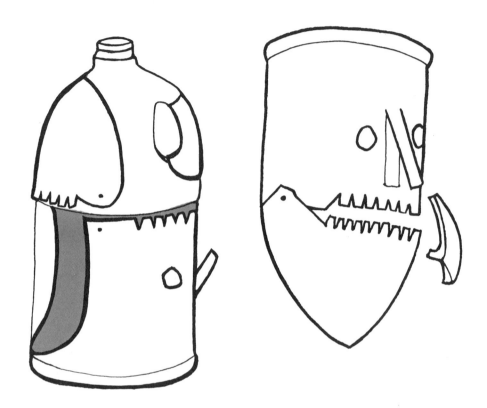

Materials & Tools: 1½ gallon plastic bleach bottle, scissors,
2 brass fasteners.

1. Cut the bottom portion of the bottle at the bulge below
   the handle.
2. Cut out the back of the bottom of the bottle.
   Cut teeth, eye holes and a nose tab.
3. Cut a lower jaw from the top portion of the bottle. Cut teeth in
   the lower jaw also.
4. Poke holes on the sides of each portion of the bottle. Use these
   holes to attach the lower jaw to the bottle head with brass
   fasteners.
5. Cut the nose from the bottle's handle. Slip it onto the nose tab.
This mask can be left white to be a scary ghost mask, or you can
color the face with markers, crayons or paint.

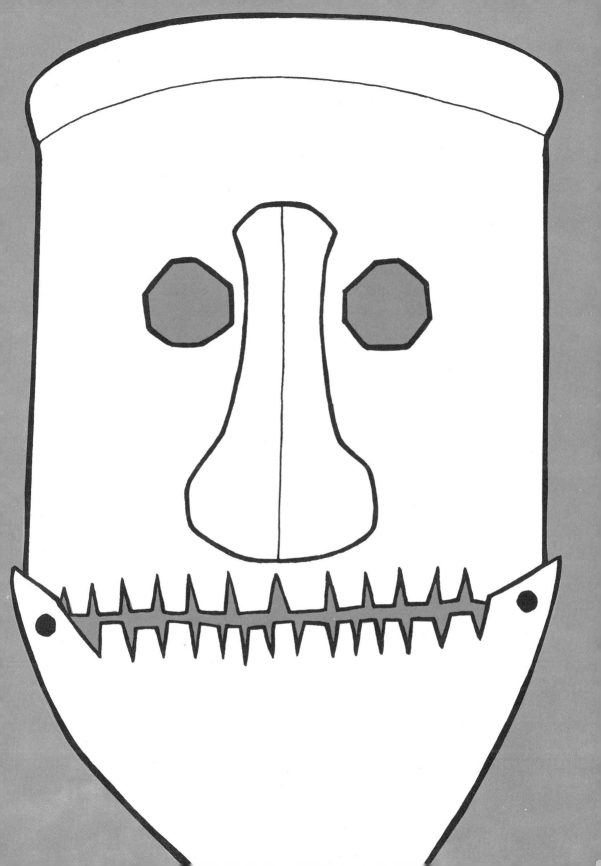

STRAW & TWINE MASK

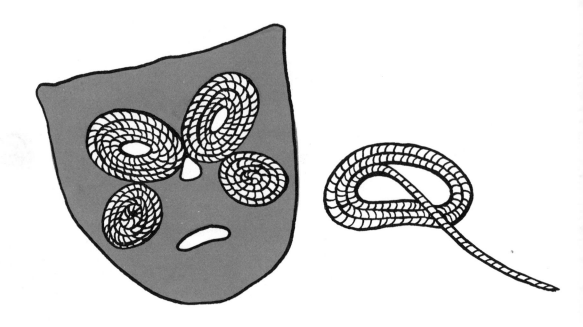

Materials & Tools: straw, twine, piece of cloth (large enough to cover your face), glue, needle and thread, scissors, plastic dairy container, beads.

1. Roll twine into 2 coils that are large enough to surround your eyes. Leave an opening in the center that is large enough for you to see out of. The coils can be sewn, stapled or taped to hold them together.

2. Cover the cloth with glue and attach the coils where your eyes will be.

3. Make other coils for cheeks and a mouth. Attach these coils to the cloth also. Leave an opening in the mouth coil.

4. Cut eye holes and a mouth opening in the cloth base.

5. Draw and cut fangs out of the dairy container. Glue them in place.

6. Sew or glue straw to attach it to the mask. Add colorful beads either to the straw or on strings hung from the mask.

FOAM RUBBER MONSTER MASK

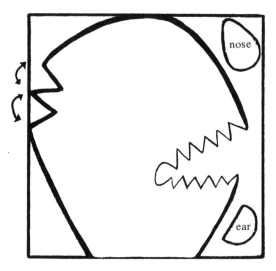

Cut the same pattern out of each piece of foam rubber. These are the 2 sides of the head.

Apply cement to heavy lines on pattern on both pieces of foam rubber. When cement is dry, join the two pieces together to foam the head.

Cut out 2 noses and cement them together, one on top of the other, for thickness. Attach the nose to the face.

Cut out 2 ears and cement them in place.

Materials & Tools: 2 pieces of 24″ square foam rubber, ½″ thick (bought in fabric stores), paper for pattern, plastic ball, yarn or fake hair, small piece of black paper or felt, pencil, scissors, glue, paint, contact cement*.

*Contact cement must be used to attach foam rubber together.

1. Copy the pattern and cut it out of paper.
2. Place the pattern on foam rubber. Cut out 2 pieces.
3. Cement the edges indicated on the pattern. Do not apply cement to the teeth or neck. Let the cement dry completely before joining the edges.
4. Copy and cut a nose and ears out of foam rubber. Cement the nose and ears in place. You must apply cement to both surfaces to be joined. Remember to let the cement dry completely before attaching pieces.
5. Paint the head a weird color. Don't paint the teeth.
6. Cut a plastic ball in half for eyes. Glue black spots cut from paper or felt in the center of each eye. Cement the eyes in place.
7. The monster can be bald or have yarn or fake hair. You can also make brows, a moustache and/or beard. Use cement to attach yarn or fake hair.

When you wear this mask, you should be able to see out of the monster's mouth.

FOIL MASKS

There are 2 types of foil, one you will find in the kitchen, and the other is bought in craft stores.

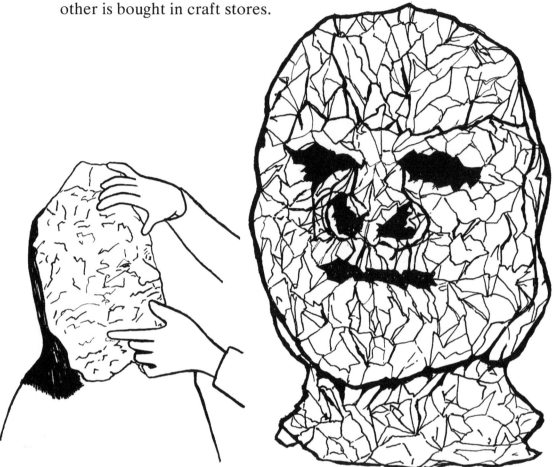

Kitchen Foil Mask

Materials & Tools: a sheet of aluminum foil at least 12″ x 30″, scissors, string.

1. Fold the sheet of foil in half. Doubled, it will measure 12″ x 15″.
2. Mold the foil over your face. Press the foil to your facial features. Keep your eyes closed. Using your finger nails, tear eye holes, nostril holes and a mouth opening. Work quickly so you can breathe easily.
3. Remove the mask from your face. Trim or fold in the extra foil at the edges. Poke holes and attach strings to the sides of the mask. This is the Metallic Monster.
4. Glue on additional pieces of foil for details or leave the mask as is.

Craft foil mask

This mask comes in copper, brass and aluminum. Copper is the easiest to work with.

Materials & Tools: foil, scissors, colored markers, ice cream stick, string.

1. Cut a mask shape. Feel and cut out eye holes.
2. Use the ice cream stick to press features and decorations into the foil.
3. Decorate the mask with colored markers.
4. Poke holes and tie strings to hold the mask on.

Additional pieces of foil can be cut, decorated and attached.

PARTIAL MASK DISGUISES

Noses

Make a paper cone nose, or use either method for papier mâché (page 30), or cloth mâché (page 32), to create a nose. Attach strings to either side and tie it on the back of your head.

Eyes and eyeglasses

Shape a pair of eyeglasses out of wire.

Cut a pair out of cardboard. Add a nose and a moustache to the cardboard glasses.

Find an old pair of glasses without lenses or a pair of sunglasses.

Bulging eyes can be made from an egg carton. Add a point from the egg carton for a nose.

Moustaches and Beards

Draw and cut a moustache out of black construction paper.

Hook it onto your nostrils or tape it on under your nose. Draw and cut a moustache and/or beard out of paper. Cut, bend and curl strips. Glue yarn or cotton on paper for a beard and moustache. Tie beards on with string.

Wigs

Use a mop,
some yarn,
a pair of tights or
panty hose,
a paper bag or
a plastic bag.
A bald head can be a swimming cap with some yarn taped to the sides.

DISGUISE HEADWEAR

Paper

A top hat is the cylinder mask (page 14) without the face portion.

A woman's hat can be made the same way, only cut shorter, and with some paper flowers glued on.

Cut out a paper crown.
Cut out a paper band and some paper feathers. Glue them on the band for an Indian headdress.

A folded piece of white paper will serve as a nurse's cap.
Hold it on with hairpins.

Cut a large round piece of paper, slit one side to the center, and tape it to create a Chinese peasant hat.

A devil's horns can be cut from an egg carton.
An angel's halo can be cut out of cardboard.

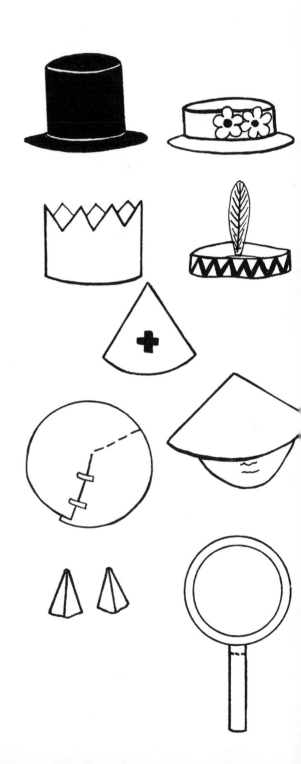

Cloth

Cut a large square from an old white sheet.

Drape it on your head.

Hold it in place with decorative cord, or twisted or braided cloth strips.

Wear dark glasses and you can disguise yourself as an Arab.

A pair of tights or panty hose with the legs wrapped around your head, can make an East Indian turban.

A plain piece of cloth can be worn over your head and covering your face below your eyes for a Moslem woman disguise.

Find a beret and be an artist.

Add a pair of sunglasses and be a star.

A bandana tied over your nose and mouth will make you a bandit.

Tie a bandana around your head, add a paper eye patch and you can be a pirate.

Complete your disguises with mother's make-up. Ask her permission to use an eyebrow pencil, some rouge and lipstick. A burnt cork is also good to make heavy eyebrows, a beard and a moustache.

About the Author/Artist

Frieda Simone Gates studied art at the Brooklyn Museum Art School, The Art Students League, The New School for Social Research and New York University. Her paintings have been exhibited in New York City, Westchester and Rockland Counties. As a professional puppeteer, she performed with the Hudson Valley Vagabound Players. Currently she is on the faculty of the art department at Rockland Community College. Mrs. Gates lives in Rockland County, New York, with her husband and their three children.